MW00743689

You Are Who You Love

For Jessica

You Are Who You Love

Using your relationships to improve yourself

T. J. Kupper

rabbit's
foot
press™

A division of Blue Mountain Arts, Inc.
Boulder, Colorado

Library of Congress Catalog Card Number: 2004017777
ISBN: 1-58786-014-7

Certain trademarks are used under license.

Printed in the United States of America.
First Printing: 2004

 This book is printed on recycled paper.

This book is printed on fine quality, laid embossed, 80 lb. paper. This paper has been specially produced to be acid free (neutral pH) and contains no groundwood or unbleached pulp. It conforms with all the requirements of the American National Standards Institute, Inc., so as to ensure that this book will last and be enjoyed by future generations.

Library of Congress Cataloging-in-Publication Data

Kupper, T. J., 1981-
You are who you love : using your relationships to improve yourself / T.J. Kupper.
        p. cm.
ISBN 1-58786-014-7 (soft cover : alk. paper) 1. Interpersonal relations. 2. Love. 3. Self-actualization (Psychology) I. Title.

HM1106.K86 2004
158.2--dc22

2004017777
CIP

Blue Mountain Arts, Inc.
P.O. Box 4549, Boulder, Colorado 80306

You Are Who You Love

Introduction 11

Step One: *Whom Do You Love?* 15

Step Two: *Finding and Analizing* 23
            Your Love Moments

Step Three: *Why Do You Love?* 37

Step Four: *Naming and Obtaining Qualities* 53

Step Five: *Becoming Who You Already Are* 63

Conclusion 73

Introduction

Yes, it's true: you really are who you love. Your relationships define you and inform you, and this book is about discovering how they can help you, as well.

You can make your own life better through looking closely at your relationships. Every time you fall in love there is a reason behind it. There is a quality or trait in that other person that draws you in. Once you can name and describe a quality or trait that each relationship represents to you, you can focus on why you admire that trait — and from there you can determine what you should be putting back into your own life. When you finish this book, you'll know yourself better and you'll know more about who you want to be — and you'll have a map for getting there.

> You can make your own life better through looking closely at your relationships.

Improving yourself by understanding your relationships is a process. I have broken this process down into a number of steps in order to make it easier to do. In step one, we will define our terms and make sure we are all starting from the same page. In steps two and three, we will look back at relationships, break them into component parts, and crystallize exactly what it was we were looking for in each relationship. In steps four and five, we will figure out how to include the desired traits in our own lives by looking to others for examples and advice.

Each section of this book includes a thought exercise that will help you stretch your memory and reclaim the most crucial moments of your life. Everything you have ever done is fair game for learning material — and your experiences will provide you with all the raw material you need to make your life better, starting today.

I will use a number of techniques to guide you on this journey. One of the methods I use is sharing a number of short anecdotes about my own life to illustrate my points and give examples. I will also guide you to make your own stories through content-based questions, set aside in a box after each story. Each section ends with a series of wrap-up questions and answers.

It is possible to read through this book and learn a lot about me from my stories, but I hope that as you read you will stay focused on yourself — your wants, needs, desires, and relationships — and what they mean to you. I will provide you with methods you can use to examine your love, your relationships, and what your behavior can mean for you. Once you achieve a higher level of self-awareness, you can use what you have learned to make your life better.

In the end, this book is about you and your life. It's about learning to look at yourself through the others *in* your life. After all, they influence you, teach you, and define you in more ways than one.

Step One:

Whom Do You Love?

*H*ave you ever found yourself wondering at a lover or a family member's ability to do something or other? Perhaps you have thought to yourself, "I wish I could be that way." Good news: you can. You can use your relationships to help you discover what is most important to you. Through this method, you will truly become more yourself by finding the parts of you that reside in others.

We have a ways to go before this will appear natural to you, so let's take it slowly. We will look deeply into past relationships and begin to analyze them. We will redefine *Moments*, *Feelings*, and *Impressions* — these are the tools we need. Then, we will discover ways of making change stick. But first, let's think about what we mean when we say we are in love.

How Do You Know?

The poets through the ages have yet to determine exactly what love is, but everyone seems to know it when they see it. Or so they claim. Some people have a very strict concept of what love is, while others have a more fluid, general understanding. In some cultures there are multiple words for different kinds of love; in other languages, love is only a noun and not a verb.

So what is love, and how do you know when you are in it?

Well, you don't, not really. You just *think* you know, and for our purposes, that's good enough. We know that love can be transitory. Everyone has heard things like, "I just don't love her anymore" or, "I fell out of love with him." If you think you are in love, then you are, at least for the moment. If you are wondering whether or not you are in love, chances are you're not.

There is no need to agonize over whether or not you love or loved a particular person. There is no limit to the number of people you can love or learn from. Nor do you need to consider the other person's love and loyalty, or the duration of the relationship. You own the love you feel, and one-way emotions

> There is no limit to the number of people you can love or learn from.

can be just as instructive as mutual relationships (though they are likely not as fulfilling).

Throughout this book, I push the idea of owning your feelings of love, for two reasons. The first is to break you of the habit of seeing love as something perfect and magical. It might be magical, but love is a human condition, and like a human, is flawed — and is therefore ripe for analysis. Breaking down the flaws into workable solutions is the whole point of this book: You are who you love, so you can examine your loves to determine who you are.

The second reason I want you to own your feelings of love is so that you can open your mind to the idea that love isn't a strictly defined thing, but a fluid and ambiguous state. As you see the diversity of the things you love, you will be able to have a better understanding of the paradox that is yourself.

How Can You Analyze Love?

When dealing with love, there is no chartable data. There are no love flow charts or graphs. Love is not measurable and is therefore incalculable. You cannot put love into a test tube and you cannot learn about yourself by measuring components of love.

Analyzing love is like analyzing a favorite movie or book or painting. It's different for every person, and it isn't about assigning numbers or using precise measuring tools. Instead, it's about examining your own feelings and reactions. You can analyze love by looking for connections among seemingly disparate pieces of information. Look for meaning in relationships as you would look for symbolism in a book: assume every detail is important and try to connect them to other events, feelings, and situations. Look for patterns. Create meanings out of the connections you draw.

I will take you through my approach to relationship analysis and show you how to create these connections in a way that is pretty simple. We'll avoid overanalyzing for two reasons: first, it wouldn't work very well — you could waste a lot of time examining every tiny detail of a relationship — and, second, a lot of the meanings you want to find in your relationships are pretty close to the surface. Those that aren't will become easier to see as you get better at this sort of introspection.

How to Find the "Main Point" of Love

To understand what is really being communicated in each of our relationships, we need to be able to simplify them. We need to take a step back from them and try to make sense out of the relationships as if they were communications aimed at teaching us something. We should treat them like we would a lecture or memo; they might have a lot of information, but to distill the most important information we should look for a main point somewhere near the beginning and a subtopic in any new section we examine. For now, we can think of the "main point" of a relationship as the Love Moment.

In each relationship there is a moment when the fact of love becomes apparent. This is not the only moment in a relationship, but it is, for all intents and purposes, the first moment in the relationship. Some brief relationships consist only of this single moment and others are more complex, but one Love Moment is the minimum requirement of any loving relationship. This moment is a central concept of this book, so I will spend the rest of the chapter going into more detail about it.

What Is the Love Moment?

First, what do I mean by a moment? A moment is the minimum duration of time in which a particular story can be contained. Just as words are the smallest elements of meaning in a sentence, a moment is the smallest unit of measurement in life.

When the love moment occurs instantaneously, they call it "love at first sight," but more often it happens some time after that. It's that moment when your heart changed its rhythm for just a second, or that time your eyes teared up as your friend walked away. It's the moment you hit the ball and found yourself looking not to your teammates, but to your dad for approval — and saw him beaming back at you.

> A moment is the minimum requirement of any relationship.

The Love Moment is a communication sent to your mind. It tells you what is going on, because while your mind is remarkably capable of knowing things and figuring them out, it can be equally remarkable in its obliviousness to your emotional and physical state. Once your mind knows you are in love, it may try to figure a course of action for you to take or words for you to say, drawing from whatever has worked for you in the past. At that point, you are also capable of learning from the love you feel.

This next story will help illustrate the moment you know you are in love.

Finding the Love Moment

I sat down on the bus and looked out the window at a blue Karmann Ghia. A girl got on and took the seat behind mine. I turned to her and remarked about the gorgeous car outside.

"Why do you say that?" asked the girl.

"It has the style of a piece of modern art: clean lines, two-tone paint job, round headlights."

We agreed cars look better with round headlights. "It gives them eyes," she said.

"I'm sorry?"

"It gives them eyes. It's easier to identify with things that have eyes." I looked through the bus seats at her eyes. Just then the car outside, the other bus riders, everything — it all disappeared.

I was saying something like, "...style for the masses — aesthetic beauty as well as practical, reliable mechanics, as evidenced by the fact that it still runs at all. What is that, the '72 model?" I was just babbling. I was talking to keep her looking at me.

"It's a '73," she corrected me.

"Is it? How can you tell?"

"You can't. Not from the outside anyway."

"Then how do you know?"

"It's mine."

How Do You Recognize the Love Moment?

This is perhaps the best kind of example for finding the Love Moment, precisely because it is such a vague situation. It isn't easy to define the Love Moment in terms of what it contains; it is easier to determine by how it feels. However, there are a few things that might help determine if a particular situation is the Love Moment.

First, trust your instincts. Love is cagey and bizarre, but you generally have a better sense of whether you are in love than you may think, and that is a great asset to you here.

Second, look at the conversation in question. The content of the conversation I just described was almost completely meaningless, and I didn't learn anything important about this girl except that she owned a cool car, which, I assure you, was not the point. What was important was that I was surprised to find out the car was hers, and I was even more surprised when, as she impressed me with her knowledge and style, I felt something I couldn't rightly describe.

A third thing to consider is focus. How is the moment focused? You may notice that the other people, the bus, even the cars disappear from the above story, and the end is just dialogue. That was how the moment played out for me. The world seemed to focus only on her and me for that moment. Think about films: whenever people fall in love in a movie, the scene will typically show a pair of close-ups, one of each person's face looking back at the other. This is pretty universal, and the reason is that the Love Moment de-emphasizes the outside world, seeming to blur it away into out-of-focus background.

The specifics of the story are totally incidental; what is important is how to recognize these kinds of world-stopping moments. They happen at truck stops and on buses and in mall parking lots as often as they do in fancy restaurants or at grand monuments. In the next chapter you'll learn to find yours, wherever they occurred, so that we can explore what they mean for you.

Questions and Answers: Step One

Whom do you love?

You love whomever you believe you love. It isn't science and it shouldn't be; don't worry too much about the difference between "like" and "love," or whether it is "real" love. None of that is important for our purposes, which are self-discovery, self-improvement, and using our relationships with other people to learn what we want and how we can get it.

How do you know love?

Sometimes you just know; maybe you find yourself surprised by someone. Maybe you see a new side of an old friend. Maybe you have just been told that someone loves you. However you realize love, the moment it becomes apparent is the Love Moment.

What is the Love Moment?

It is the moment you realize there is love: that you have love for someone, they have love for you, or you have love for each other. The Love Moment is an epiphany. It is hard to get down on paper exactly how it feels, because there is always a physical component that is difficult to locate and differs from person to person. But you physically feel that something exists between you and someone else, something that cannot be seen or pinpointed.

Okay, I understand the Love Moment. But I don't know what I love about people. How am I supposed to determine why I love someone?

The trick to determining why you love someone starts with the Love Moment, but it doesn't end there. When you are in love, it happens for certain reasons, and if you can get at those reasons, you can find some surprising and revealing things about yourself. You will see things in other people that you wish you had, traits they possess that you don't, and manners in which they do things that you envy. You will be able to connect these attributes back to yourself, learn from them, and use them to help you improve your life. We are going to spend the next several chapters dealing with this exploration.

Step Two:

Finding and Analyzing Your Love Moments

*I*n step one, we adopted a broad definition of love, but the fact of its existence, at least from your own perspective, is what must reveal itself in the Love Moment. I've already shown you an example of a Love Moment, so I think you have a good idea of what they are. Now it is time for you to find some of your own.

You can find the Love Moments in your life anywhere: in obvious settings, such as an intimate discussion, or in ones that are more subtle and obscure. Both are equally likely to occur, and it really is up to chance. If you trust yourself, you will know when it occurs. As you remember past experiences, look for the following things: physical exhilaration, changes in focus, surprising information, and revelatory statements. These are clues that the moment you are remembering might be the Love Moment.

Think about how our language describes the process of becoming in love: you *fall* in or out of love. Love then, by implication, is involuntary. It is a tiger trap in the jungle, unexpected and undeniable. You fall into it and you are stuck — until the trap flips over and you fall out again.

That's useful for us. Think about the Love Moment as a connection made without effort — though not necessarily without intention. Keep in mind that your definition of love should be fairly broad: familial relations, close friends, and significant others of various kinds — boyfriends to wives, lovers to soul mates — are all fair game. You should feel free to look closely at past relationships you've had, rather than feeling limited to your spouse or current flame. You can learn as much from negative experiences as from positive ones. The reasons that relationships work or fail are fascinating doors to self-awareness.

When you are looking for the Love Moment, focus very sharply on the way you feel about the exchange you remember. This is the truest indication of whether you are looking at a "real" Love Moment.

The following is an exercise to help you define and relive Love Moments from your life.

Experiencing the Moment

There are a number of ways to relive a moment, but first you have to pick the moment you want to relive. Some people find this easy. They choose the first time they fell in love, or the last time they were truly and completely overjoyed with another person's presence. If you have trouble locating one, try this:

- Pick a relationship you want to remember. Who were you with when you were first experiencing something important? Was it the date to your senior prom? Your first college romance? Or maybe a summer fling?
- When did you first meet? When did you last see one another? Was there something that happened when your relationship changed from friendship to something else?
- Once you've decided on a moment, lean back, close your eyes (after you finish reading this, of course), and re-enact the moment in your head. Feel free to talk, move your hands, or get up and walk around the room if it helps, but relive the whole scene as if you were an actor rehearsing it.
- Now form it into a story. Write it down, and only tell what is absolutely essential to know. Limit yourself to one page of small type or two of handwriting. If you don't like to write, at least be able to answer the following questions:
- *When does the moment start?* What is the absolute earliest time that makes sense for starting the story?
- *What happens?* What's the plot of your memory?
- *How does it end?* What do you realize? When do you know the moment is over?
- You knew you were in love when this moment ended. Why? What were you in love *with?*

You can master the ability to isolate and describe moments in this way. Try to grasp a moment that sums up each major event or time period in your life: the shift from elementary to middle school, puberty, your first day of high school, your last day of college, your first long-term relationship, your wedding day, the day your first child was born, etc. Follow the above exercise for as many different moments as you need to start feeling comfortable thinking about and telling stories about those you have loved.

Composite Moment Phenomenon

When did you first realize you loved your mother? Can you make that moment replay itself in your head? Probably not. Sometimes a moment is a conflation of two or more events or actions. I call this Composite Moment Phenomenon. The facts may need to be fixed a little in order to make sense of the seemingly random way the real world's events occur.

Maybe you see an amazing sight with a person and you remember a conversation you had days or months before, and together the two things create a special meaning for you. That is your moment; don't worry too much about being perfectly accurate to the way it happened in real life. Accuracy isn't the most important thing.

The important thing in this exercise is to focus on the meaning of the relationship *to you*. Perhaps the person taught you something about the world. If so, what was the form of the lesson? Perhaps you saw a side of someone no one else sees. How would you tell your friend about it if you only had one minute to tell the story and they had to understand the first time?

Moments can be an elusive concept, so let's think about some pivotal times in our lives and the moments that defined them. I'll take you through some experiences I consider to be life changing, and you should think about those rite-of-passage times in your life. Remember to think about

Sometimes a moment is a conflation of two or more events or actions.

who you were with, what the person said, and how you interacted with them — your moments will come back to you.

Making New Friends

In the first week of my freshman year of high school, I attended a club meeting to try to make some new friends.

One place of confidence for me was art class, so I decided to go to a weekly art club I'd heard about. When I got to the club, one of the kids was the older sister of a girl I knew. She was an artist and a junior. She painted, sculpted, drew — everything. I could draw a cartoon okay, but I knew nothing about paint or clay. To me, her work looked completely professional. Her name was Lynn.

She approached me. She showed me the self-portrait she was working on and asked to see my drawings. I sheepishly passed over my page of doodles. They were pathetic compared to hers, but she pointed at the best one on the page, laughed, and told me it was good.

The art club was not a social clique. People there cared about their work, but they didn't define themselves by it. I was apprehensive about giving myself a confining social label — joining the jocks or the drama club or whatever — but Lynn had no so such affiliation.

"What are you?" I asked her, anxious to know how I could avoid being pigeonholed.

"I'm not anything but me," she said. "Don't worry about what other people call you. It only limits you. Don't let it."

Different Kinds of Love

I found a role model in Lynn, a person who exemplified the inclusive and honest person I wanted to be. She was adamantly herself and talented, too. It wasn't romance, but it was love. I needed something and she was able to provide it for me. I felt I could know her well and learn from her. I felt she was willing to learn from me.

Close friendships and romantic relationships both have the same potential for self-discovery. Of course, there is a difference between platonic and romantic love, but the feeling of being with good, loved friends is just as good as the feeling of being with romantic lovers, and the things you see in both groups are valuable as you try to discover what you want.

I was able to learn about myself from what I liked about Lynn. My feeling when I was with her wasn't the same as a romantic vibe, but it was just as positive and strong. I was able to find out what made me feel that vibe by thinking back on our moments together — and I used that to learn about myself.

Finding Your Own Moments

When you are in a new social interaction, what qualities do you look for? Why?

What makes you feel comfortable in a group? Is it the way a leader of the group acts? Or the way the group members interact? What makes you feel at home? What makes you think you can act as they do, or that your actions and theirs are compatible?

Can you remember a time when you were first in a new place, like a school or job? How did you make friends or choose a group? This can let you know what you look for in these situations. Maybe you look for a group with strict rules so that you have a code of conduct while you get used to new routines. Maybe you prefer an amorphous group structure because you don't like authority.

When Moments Seem Inevitable

Some moments happen during life's turning points. Turning points are high-stress and highly examined and as a result seem to create moments. Don't be surprised if you find several moments around stressful times: weddings and funerals, childbirth, prom, college. It's natural.

Love moments that occur during these times can seem exaggerated or unusually vivid. There is frequently an intensity surrounding a turning point memory that is rare — and is helpful for our purposes. The memories that seem to glow in your mind will be easy to isolate and extrapolate from.

Take, for example, this next story. It describes a cursory, not particularly intimate relationship. But the intensity of the experience was so heightened by its happening while I was a foreign-exchange student in Tokyo that it stays with me very clearly. Perhaps this is because it came at a turning point in my life, a time when I was farther away than ever before from all the people I knew and loved.

A Moment of Departure

Yoshiko stared across the bay, her eyes fixed on a point in the distance. I looked around me, and took in the white bridge filled with commuters, the throngs of beachgoers, the crowds surging from place to place. Tokyo was a fast and dense city and I, with little language ability and less energy, was overwhelmed. I watched a thousand cars' headlights crawling across the Rainbow Bridge.

"You see that star?" Yoshiko asked.

I nodded. "Wait. What? I was looking at the headlights."

"I was looking at that star," she said, pointing. The Tokyo sky is polluted with light so not many stars come through, but across the bay, the sky in Yokohama was darker and one bright, red star shone.

"It looks like a headlight," I mumbled.

"I was looking at it, and I was thinking," she began, looking for the English, "how lucky we are to be young. There is so much for us that is possible. We can do what we want, be who we want. The people on that bridge, stuck in their cars, have to look at headlights. We can look at stars. We could spend all night looking for them." She turned then and looked at me.

"I suppose you are right."

Look for the Long View

Yoshiko could look around her and easily see positive things. I am by nature more cynical, so it was a shock for me to hear her. Sometimes I thought her naïve, but mostly I admired the way she saw the world.

I knew I was in the Love Moment because the world again focused down and the headlights and stars kind of disappeared while she talked. But I was also far from home and, for the first time, realizing something about someone who was as different from me as I imagined a person could be. This turning point virtually ensured that this moment would seem very important to me. And it was — I learned something.

Your preferences come from you and are therefore already part of you.

I felt a deep sense of appreciation in Yoshiko, a knowing naïveté that I was able to apply to my situation. I could find ways of thinking more positively by imagining what she would say about them. I could be more appreciative just by putting myself in her mindset, which I would not have been able to do if I hadn't known her. Without fundamentally changing my idea of myself, I was able to approximate the kind of appreciative attitude that I was looking for.

As you continue to search for your Love Moments, you'll find that you start to think this way automatically. Your loved ones become like voices on your shoulder that you can listen to if you like.

I think what Yoshiko said about headlights and stars can apply to the subject of this book as well. Headlights and stars are always around you, but if you can look up from your car at the sky, you are likely to find something more meaningful. When you think back on your relationships, try not to look at headlights. Look for the long view. When you find a moment in your memory, imagine it as a star. Not rare, perhaps, but special anyway — a thing of wonder, of great value.

You have two choices: you can sit in traffic, staring at headlights, or you can reach for that star. Each star-bright memory you have is a Love Moment. And each one can help you become the person you most want to be.

Finding Your Own Moments

Have you ever been alone somewhere? In a foreign country maybe, or just in a situation that felt totally alien? The people you cling to in such situations can tell you a lot about how you want to handle your life.

In any group of people you will always feel more comfortable around some people than others. Why? What makes these people seem safe? Is it just that they are like you, or is it something else? Are they, in fact, like you?

Remember that when you are choosing others, you are choosing yourself, too — you are looking for your ideal self among the various real people around you.

Where You Are Coming From

Before we move on, I have to mention that your family is a large determining factor in who you are. You love your family as well as your friends and lovers, so they are also an excellent source of moments and realizations.

Understanding the bonds of family is an integral part of self-knowledge. Knowledge of who you are and where you come from is central to grasping a sense of yourself as an individual who is unique, yet who also comes from a specific environment that has shaped you quite a lot. If you look at yourself that way and define both how you are different from your family and what it means to be a member of your family, you can do two things: one, you can challenge the central concepts of your life that don't help you, and two, you can start to trace some of the better things in your personality to their points of origin. This, in turn, can point you to more good things you can adopt.

What I mean by challenging the concepts that don't help you is this: Look into your family history and the things that you consider essential to yourself because they run in your family. Inevitably, some of it is just habit. You are intolerant, perhaps, because your dad is, or you learned to be impatient from your mom. This is likely something you hear a lot at family gatherings: "So-and-so is just like someone else because he does this thing."

If you examine these qualities, you will realize that you have a lot more control over them than you think. Relationships can illuminate that. Think about a time in your life when, for whatever reason, you acted fundamentally different from the way you act in your "normal life": maybe your first year away at college or at summer at camp. You can also contrast your business manner with the way you deal with your friends. Why do you change your behavior in these times? Because of the people around you.

You are a product of your surroundings, but the things you learned from your family may be specific to your family and may not help you in your current situation. On the other hand, remembering family members, especially those you don't see often, is a great way to pick up new good habits.

The Limitations of Family Relationships

So why not just focus on your parents and forget about dealing with other kinds of love to learn about yourself? Your relationship with your parents is complex and helpful, but it is limited, too.

As you grow, your parents become your standards for values like generosity, responsibility, common sense, and really almost everything. This can be a problem. It's not that they are wrong, but there is a whole world of possibilities out there, and many of them may work better in certain circumstances. You have to judge critically for yourself. That is why it is so important to include all the people you love, with all their differences, when you are looking to discover and change yourself.

Finding Your Own Moments

Try to see yourself as distinct from your family. What things do all members of your family do that you do, too? What differs between you and the group?

Can you remember when you first did something that shocked your family? Or when you first did something consciously different from the example your family set? Why did you do that?

Questions and Answers: Step Two

I can think of an important moment in my relationship with a particular person, but it wasn't anywhere near the beginning of the relationship. What should I do about that?

That is good; you are skipping ahead to next chapter, when the temporal location of the moment will become much less important. I want you to focus on Love Moments — which are mostly near the beginning of a relationship — because I think they are the easiest to grasp and to remember, but if you are finding other kinds of moments, then that means you are getting the concepts and moving ahead.

I think I have chosen a Love Moment, but I'm not sure. How do I know?

Unfortunately there is no siren. You just have to trust yourself and make a decision. Try thinking about why you're uncertain. Is it because you aren't sure that you felt love or because you are unsure of something else, like what it means to admit you love that person, or how many people you have loved, or whether that person loved you? Those should not be criteria. Only your love matters in determining the Love Moment. Did you feel love? If not, what was it?

So by Composite Moment Phenomenon, can I make up anything to make the moment work?

Not quite. You can't make things up; look hard and you'll find that the real, true stories are there and ready to be used. The stories you make up from your own imagination are likely a better window into what you would like to have happen, or are perhaps afraid of having happen, rather than who you are. But they can still tell you something about yourself. If you have a great urge to make up a story, ask yourself why that is. Do you not want to remember a painful past experience? Or are you uncomfortable with reliving that foolish time? What is holding you back?

If my whole family acts a certain way, why would I want to be different?

Your family is a huge determinant in who you are, but individual traits that you have picked up are probably more related to habit and example than nature. You can use this as a departure point for bringing good things into your life and for clearing space for more good things by recognizing bad habits and working to eliminate them.

One of the easiest ways to eliminate a bad habit is to find a good counterexample and stick to that. For example, if you are disgusted by your little brother's tactless way of talking, you might focus on how your cousin speaks so politely to adults. Or if your whole family has a tendency to cut people off when they talk, you might concentrate on imitating a good listener you used to date whenever someone talks to you.

What is different about analyzing my relationship with my parents and my relationships with others?

You sublimate your parents without study. Those people with whom you've had less contact are easier to step away from, but harder to pin down. It may be hard to step back far enough from your parents to learn from them, but it will be rewarding to do so. Meanwhile, some of your more easily understood relationships may not teach you as much precisely because they are less complex and therefore reveal more simple, surface-level things about you, but they are easier to access and will be useful practice toward making bigger realizations.

Step Three:

Why Do You Love?

Whenever you fall in love, you fall in love with a quality or trait. You fall in love with it for one of three reasons:

- A: You admire those who do what you think you cannot do.
- B: You admire those who do what you do, but better.
- C: You admire those who confirm your choices by making the same ones.

More simply, you like people because they *are* like you (C), they are like you but *better* somehow (B), or because they are *not* like something you *dislike* in yourself (A). You can learn from possibilities B and C, but the most instructive and most common reason for attraction is reason A.

Before you can discover what you need to learn from each of these types of relationships, you must also be able to name the qualities and traits in question. To do that, you need to break relationships down into component parts that can be inspected. We've already determined that the beginning of each relationship is a moment. You can think of each relationship as simply a collection of moments, experienced over time.

Moment by Moment

Try to consider each relationship in terms of the instructive moments you've experienced through your connection with the other person. Each relationship you have is an opportunity to learn something. The moments you distill are the lessons. Try to see your life as a chain of moments, each a small revelation. These commonplace epiphanies are the basis of a relationship-centered introspection, and the next step in becoming who you love.

Remember: A perfect way to learn about ourselves is to look at other people. By focusing on the actions and statements that cause us to feel love, we can find the things that are, by definition, most important to us.

Take your relationship with a parent. Perhaps you can remember a number of moments from childhood in which your parent impressed you, accomplished something seemingly impossible, or helped you accomplish something you couldn't do alone. These moments are part of the relationship, as are the moments when you realized your parent was a flawed and limited person or when you found out that your parent was once young like you. These moments together add up to the impression you have of your parent.

Perhaps you can remember a number of moments from childhood in which your parent impressed you, accomplished something seemingly impossible, or helped you to accomplish something you couldn't do alone.

Each moment contains its own arc, but there is a larger arc to the relationship itself, and that is what I am calling an impression. If you take the moments of any one relationship together, you can create a composite impression that defines the relationship for you.

From this point, you can proceed by naming the impression, and then you can begin to learn from this relationship. Here is a simple example from my own life.

In the Air

Rose and I were wandering around a park after sundown. It had a school playground on one side and a pond on the other. We came upon the playground and got up on the swings. For an hour she swung breathlessly next to me. We said nothing. I sat in the swing and marveled at her good time.

She eventually realized I wasn't swinging and asked why I didn't swing, too. I didn't have an answer for her. It hadn't occurred to me. But she looked flushed and happy, so I gave it a try. After a few tugs I was high up, swinging better than I could remember doing as a child. Then she was in the air next to me.

Half an hour later, she jumped off and I followed her. We scrambled across the jungle gym, down the slide, up the ladders, and down the pegs. Finally exhausted, we lay on our backs, sweat dripping off our hair onto the earth, and she turned to me and said, "Isn't it funny what we have to do just to enjoy a little cold, wet grass?"

Impressions from Moments

This moment summed up my interactions with Rose; during all our time together she seemed to show me the same thing in different ways. The moment exemplifies the impression that I got, one of simple *wonder*, which I recognized but had lost. She showed me how I could remain full of wonderment. This has allowed me to enjoy life more deeply without losing focus.

I began to practice Rose's method; I allowed myself, when with her, to enjoy the things that she enjoyed so naturally. And when we weren't hanging out together, I still felt freer to stop and smell the roses.

Finding Your Own Moments

Meeting Rose would have changed me whenever it was, but being young helped me to remain open to her ideas. Try to reconnect with the ideas you were presented with in young romances. Were these silly, meaningless notions? Some of them surely have bearing on your life now.

If you cannot name the impression of a relationship, perhaps the relationship is too complex to be contained by a single impression. Complex relationships are harder to make sense of and are often contradictory over time. Remember to keep yourself in focus when thinking about this kind of relationship. What things most affected and stayed with you? Those are the most important. Figure the contradictions out in a way that makes sense for you to learn positive things from the other person.

Impressions as a Series of Moments

For an example of how to analyze a more complicated relationship, I turn to my parents. In their case, the overall impression is much too complex to be encapsulated in a single word or moment. The moments group together in many different ways, making many different impressions. But I can take each impression that comes to mind as a distinct and separate instance, as if each comes from a totally different person.

Here is an example of one impression I found in each of my parents. They don't circumscribe the relationships entirely, but they illuminate individual parts that are small enough to learn from.

"Audio Dad"

My father taught me how to listen to music. Over a period of time he would put music on and sit me down, telling me to focus on various parts of the sound mix and explaining what was happening technically. I learned to distinguish different types of studio effects, guitars, guitar amplifiers, and various other instruments upon hearing them. Soon I had a trained ear, and now I can't listen to music without automatically taking it apart and reconstructing it in my head. Any new sound immediately makes me try to distinguish how it was made and what was done in recording it to give it the quality it has.

These moments create an impression of my relationship with my dad, that I call Audio Dad. Audio Dad is a distinct impression and set of lessons based on those times he taught me about music. It is completely separate from the many other impressions I have of my father, such as Auto Advice Dad or Tennis Playing Dad. I learned from each one, and each taught me something different.

Audio Dad never said, "This is how to listen to music." He'd say, "Listen to this bass line — you hear that? Listen to that and how it turns around...." You learn from your parents by doing, talking, and trying things.

"Relationship Advice Mom"

My mother also has many different modes of behavior, and each creates a distinct impression in my head. Relationship Advice Mom is a much more helpful, sympathetic, and rational person than, say, Concerned About My Safety Mom. Relationship Advice Mom was the one who first taught me to use logic to analyze relationships. She never sat me down and said, "This is how you analyze relationships," but it was from my mother that I learned the difference between analysis and over analysis, which is an important part of the method I am showing you.

We all have a tendency to deconstruct every action of other people, looking for communicative meaning: "He said *this* at lunch, which means he *likes* me, but he held his pencil between his first and second fingers in study hall, which means he *doesn't*." If that sounds immature, that's because it is. Most human action doesn't have an intentional, communicative meaning behind it. Maybe it is true, for example, that people who like each other will absently cross their legs toward each other, but that sort of thing only works if the people involved aren't thinking about it. You have to be careful not to assign meaning to meaningless events, but on the other hand try to be watchful of all that occurs.

Learn to analyze your relationships logically but not obsessively, as if they were elements of a song, movie, or other artwork. The multiple impressions you get from each relationship, like different songs by the same artist, will likely be related, but each can teach you something distinct and important.

Why Learn from Others?

It's very hard to look at yourself objectively; some might say it is impossible. And while it is often difficult to be totally objective about those you are close to, you can get some distance when thinking about them. If you were able to look inside yourself and find a list of things that add up to "You," you wouldn't need this book.

You can find yourself by paying close attention to how you deal with other people. In others you see yourself reflected and you gravitate toward things that fit you naturally. These things are already a part of you and, with simple and easy introspection, can become powerful, positive forces in your life. That is why we need to look to others to find ourselves: we choose others based on who we are, and because we fall in love instinctively, our loves are a fantastically accurate window into who we really are, not who we think we should be, who we pretend to be, or who others think we are.

There are other options for kinds of people to study: celebrities or people you don't know, for example, but that is likely to lead to very superficial analysis. You can look into fictional characters, and this can be useful, but it also has limited usefulness because real-world situations are very different from fictional ones, and your situation is specific to you.

The beauty of this methodology is that it is based entirely on you and what your life is like: the people you meet are a product of your surroundings, and they are as diverse or particular as your experience. Thus the realizations you make while reading this book will automatically apply directly to your life, because your life is their source. The lessons come from you, are defined by you, and are, in that way, ideally suited to help you.

Extending the Concept

You can use this kind of technique to look at anything. It isn't necessarily even limited to people, but I think that the realization "I like Bauhaus furniture" just isn't as impressive or useful as "I want to be more attuned to wonder."

Remember that love shouldn't be limited just to romantic situations: good friends and family are excellent sources to inspire your self-reflection. The same logic applies: Look for things in the person you like, then try to apply those traits to your own life. Here is an example of learning from friendly, non-romantic love.

True Faith

Amanda sat on a shady bench in the center of campus, and I sat on the ground next to her feet. I asked her what was the most important thing in her life.

"My relationship with God."

"Really?"

"Why? What's most important to you?"

"Art."

"How can you say that?"

"Well, art is there to comfort me when I am alone. Art gives me examples of how I can live my life, but ultimately lets me make my own choices. Art can't be controlled by any one person or group, and it is a culmination of all the thought and energy of the people around me. Art offers possibilities for meaning in my life, and art gives me a vocabulary and a method to use when I look for meaning. Art tells me who I am and that my story can have value to others. And, because I can create art, it gives me a chance to give back."

She looked down on me with a kind smile. "Art is everything to you?"

"Art is a window onto human possibility."

"So is God."

"Art speaks to me."

"God speaks to me. God gives me examples of how I can live my life, but ultimately lets me make my own choices. God can't be controlled by any one person or group and is a culmination of all the thought and energy of the people around me. God offers possibilities for meaning in my life, and God gives me a vocabulary and a method to use when I look for meaning. God tells me who I am and that my story can have value to others."

"But you can't create your own God."

"No, but God is what we make of Him."

"So is Art."

Have You Ever Seen Similarity in Difference?

Amanda had true faith, and through her I realized that my beliefs weren't very different from hers. The two systems were compatible. The moment of love, though, came in the recognition of similarity in difference. Amanda and I could believe different things, but it was her capacity to believe that I admired. I also had that capacity, but too often I didn't allow myself the luxury of developing it.

The love I felt for Amanda was spiritual. It wasn't romantic love, but it felt like we had shared something important, more than friends usually do. We had opened a sensitive part of ourselves to one another and found understanding, though not agreement. Sharing your beliefs with someone is definitely a kind of expression of love; it is personal and potentially damaging information that might make you self-conscious. When you choose to share that information, think about what makes you want to do it.

Finding Your Own Moments

When in your life have your beliefs been most tested? Was it by someone you loved? Could you love someone with different beliefs? Why or why not? Try to connect your beliefs to your love. How are they related?

Now think about your own faith and where it came from. Can you trace it back to a single moment or influential person? Or is it a habit you grew up with? Do you share your faith with others?

Who gets to know about your beliefs? Why them? What makes you trust them with this information? What about that person makes you feel comfortable enough to share?

Feelings and Names

Now that you've had some experience analyzing relationships and finding love moments, take your impression of one relationship you've thought of. What would you name it? Think of an emotion. See if there is one feeling that seems like a fitting title.

You have to be able to define your feelings in order to accurately think about and compare experiences. Everyone feels various emotions, and there are a lot of words out there to describe them. You can use any that fit, but be able to define the words you use.

Once you can create an impression in your mind of what a relationship means for you, you can give it a name. I try to use the impression in the title of the moments I write about. I try to use the name to remind me what I cared about in the relationship in the first place.

This naming will help you succeed as you become who you love. Naming things is the first step toward wanting them, and wanting them is the first step toward getting them.

Try the following exercise to help you learn to define your feelings.

Impression Into Feeling

- To define a feeling, try to describe it to yourself. What happens, physically, when you think of the moments that make up your relationship? The impression you get has an effect on you. There are also associations you can make, like: "The only other time I have felt that way was when...."
- You already know how to relive a moment. Try reliving several from the same relationship. You don't have to write these down; just think about them. Pay close attention to what happens to your facial features as you do this. Are you smiling? Is your brow furrowed? Are your muscles tense or relaxed? When your concentration is somewhere else, your face is an excellent indicator of how you are feeling.
- Feelings are hard to put into words. Maybe you can think of a story, movie, or song that expresses what you are thinking. Focus on this particular piece of art. What is its message? What part of it recalls your relationship? Why?
- If the answer to one of the above is not a feeling, try this. Get a piece of paper and write a letter to the person you are thinking of. Explain what they mean to you, why you love them, and what you want from them. When you are done, read the letter over. What are you really trying to say? Read the letter as if you had received it from someone else — what would it tell you?
- Once you have gotten the hang of naming relationships by feeling and impression, try making a long list of first names of people you have loved. Next to each name write down two words: the impression in the first column and the feeling in the second. Remember, the impression is the collective description of the moments of the relationship, and the feeling you admired or envied in the loved person is the feeling you should write down.

Here is a story from my own life that may help you learn to connect impressions to feelings.

The Alphabet Backwards

My sister thought it would be fun to teach me how to read one day, so she called me downstairs. She was a teacher at heart and had on numerous earlier occasions forced me to recite whatever sort of rote knowledge she had learned at school that day, so I already knew state capitals, important dates in U.S. history, easy math tables, and more. But now she decided I needed language.

"Okay," she started, "recite the vowels."

I did: "A, E, I, O, U, and sometimes Y."

"Okay, now recite the consonants. Backwards."

"Z and Y and X, uh, W, V, U — "

"No!"

"W, V, T — "

"No, start again from the beginning," she said, though she actually meant to start again from the end.

This went on. By the end of it I could do the whole lot of them, backwards, forwards, with or without vowels, with or without song. And not too long after, I found that I could read.

Who Is Your Standard of Experience?

Let me explain how I use moments like this from my relationship with my sister to name the impression I have of her. She was always the most knowledgeable person I knew whose experience was close enough to mine that I could ask her advice or look to her for an example. She had knowledge, which I learned was different from intelligence. Everyone seemed to think I was smart, but as to how much I knew, it was clear that I would have to learn a lot to catch up to this girl who had six years of life on me.

The impression I got from my sister was that she was knowledgeable and in command. Her ability to call out right or wrong — and her knowledge that I cared — gave her immense power. It was one thing to be smart, but I realized right away that if I were going to have any power at all, I would need to have a great deal of knowledge as well. I wanted a feeling of power, and I realized through her that knowledge was the way to get it. The impression was of knowledge; the feeling was of *awe* at the power she held. And she was the key to learning I wanted that power myself.

It is impossible to tell someone how to name a thing; the process is an automatic one while thinking. You might have an easy time remembering who was your standard of a "knowledgeable" person at a young age, and if so, maybe you can see what I mean. If not, though, you can look for other kinds of impressions.

Finding Your Own Moments

Can you remember admiring someone else's power in any way? A boss at work, or a kid at school who was always placed in charge of things? Or perhaps a teacher? These people had something you wanted — power — and they gave you an impression that seemed to justify it. Name the impression.

Maybe your boss made you fear him because he always gave the impression of having his mind made up. His stubbornness discouraged you from disagreeing with him. Or perhaps your girlfriend was so encouraging of your work that you always felt you could do great things when you were with her. Maybe a teacher amazed you by always seeming to have everything organized down to the smallest detail, while you naturally winged most assignments. These all count as impressions. Find some of your own.

Questions and Answers: Step Three

So wait: why do I love?

You love because you found something to love in the other person. That's what this chapter is all about: isolating and naming the things that attract you to others. Think back on the people you trust and those you have clung to in times of crisis and watershed moments. Remember your parents and siblings, your first love, your prom date, and your college sweetheart. Remember these people and start to look for the moments in the relationships.

Once you have found the moments, name the impression you got from that person, or in other words, the thing you loved. If that is elusive, answer this: What does their presence represent to you? There is meaning there and you can find it.

Once you have it, you have to give it a name. By now you should be able to make a long list of names of people you have loved, and next to each name you should be able to write down a single word that describes how you feel (or felt) when near them. Try using the techniques in the *Impression Into Feeling* exercise (page 47), or try something else that works for you. Why are these people important to you? What feelings do they bring you?

All the people I love are nothing like me. What does that mean?

Remember the three reasons we love someone. Reason C is that people may be unlike you in a way you feel you aren't able to be, but desire to be. But you must realize that you won't fall in love with things that you cannot be; you are who you love, and you are *what* you love about these seemingly very different people. You can become what they are because, as you will see, you are already it.

We'll talk more about that in step five, but for now, ask yourself: What are the important moments of my relationship? What impression do I get that made me love this person? And what feeling do I have when he/she is around that I don't have otherwise?

Even if, as far as you can tell, the person you love is everything you hate, there must be some reason you feel that love. Pay close attention to the particulars of your relationship, distill moments, impressions from moments, and feelings from impressions. You will find it.

I can think of feelings others inspire without all this moment mumbo jumbo!

Good. This book assumes nothing; I'm outlining techniques that work for me. The idea will still help you whether or not you need all the techniques. If you are having no trouble following along, you can skip ahead or just read without stopping to follow the exercises.

Naming and Obtaining Qualities

*B*y now, you can look at your relationships as a series of instructive moments, each revealing a little bit about what you need and want. You can look at complex relationships as impressions developed from a series of moments over time, informing you of what you look for in others and what you are deterred by, as well.

You have some practice naming the feelings that are the result of these impressions and moments, but feelings are vague and hard to grasp. In order to discover something really useful, something you can put into your own life, you need to pinpoint a quality that you either have and need more of or don't have but want to acquire.

So how do you make the jump from feeling something to expressing it? In time, it will become automatic, but we can speed the process along with a technique I call Naming Things.

In order to get at something really useful, something you can put into your own life, you need to pinpoint a quality that you either have and need more of or don't have but want.

Naming Things

Naming things is an invaluable lesson to learn, because you must learn to name things if you ever hope to get them. This technique is a product of the methods I have outlined so far. It should help you recognize how to distill helpful things out of your own relationships. It will also help you acquire the knack for naming things that is going to be essential for you to articulate and achieve your newfound goals.

By now you are a pro at telling simple short stories, right? You can easily distill a moment down to its simplest details and then, by looking at those details, you can find the name it needs. A quality or trait is nothing more than a description, so if you imagine you only have one word with which to describe your partner to a stranger, you will find that quality.

It isn't the same as naming a feeling because the feeling you get with someone is not a description of the person. This is the one-word version of why you fell in love with this person. It can be a state: wonder. Or it can be a trait: adventurousness. Or it can be a personality quality: strength. The following exercise is designed to help you name things.

Naming Exercise

Take the list of people's names you made in the last chapter. Next to each one, make a fourth column and use the techniques outlined to create a single-word description of the quality that person had that made you love them. Remember, there might have been many lovable things about them, but one was most important. One thing made it inevitable, inescapable. There was one thing that, all else being different, would have still undoubtedly made you fall for this person. That is the thing you most need. That is the name you are looking for.

Naming Things: Karen's Pluck

Once in the high school library, as I sat reading a book, I noticed a girl across the room looking in my direction. I smiled, and she looked away. I turned back to my book and didn't see her leave her seat and come closer. She tapped me on the shoulder, and when I looked back, she had a sheepish grin. She asked, "Do you have a pencil?" I looked at her backpack. It had two pencils, the sharp ends sticking out of the small front pocket.

"No, I don't. But you do." I pointed to her bag, and as she looked down, I saw her cheeks turn red. "What's your name?"

"Karen."

"Well, Karen, why don't you sit down and talk to me?"

Have You Ever Just Gone for It?

If I had to explain Karen in a single word, I would say Karen had "pluck." You could also call it "confidence," or "verve." I fell for her ability to go for what she wanted. The fact was, she came over to me with nothing; she clearly had two pencils and hadn't even bothered to hide them. But the message — "I want to talk to you" — came through loud and clear.

In the confusion of high school, forthrightness can be an asset. In her roundabout way, Karen was naming what she wanted.

Finding Your Own Moments

The things you learned from a high school romance, no matter how confusing they may have been at the time, can stay with you long after.

Think back on a romance you had with someone you first met in high school. What drew you to them? Would that still attract you now? If so, think about what you could do to bring that into your life now. For my part, I try not to worry about having an entry line anymore — I just let the person I'm talking to know that I want to talk to them more than I want to say a particular thing. What do you do?

If you think that the attraction would no longer be there, think about why. What is different in your life now? How is life now fundamentally different from high school so that this is no longer a desirable trait? How would the trait have to change to apply to your life now?

Owning Your Love

Love is supposed to be a two-way street, a compromise, a selfless state of perfect harmony. Right?

As anyone living outside a fairy tale knows, love is not anywhere near as perfect as that. Love can be jealous, selfish, demanding, and manipulative — but it is also the best thing we have found here on earth, so we'll take it however we can get it. One important part of my method is to dispense with fairy tale notions of love.

You should see love as something you own. It is not important, for instance, whether the people you love return that love (at least not for the purposes of this book, which are self-knowledge and self-improvement). Your love for them is what will help you become more self-aware and improve *your* life. Maybe you loved a person because of her sense of wonder, as I did. This indicates you miss that sense of wonder in your life, or wish you had more of it.

This is the center of using relationships as a departure point for self-discovery. You have to remember that who you love says quite a lot about you — maybe even more about you than about the other person. That's the point of owning your love: it belongs to you, and what's important is what it means for you.

> Who you love says quite a lot about you — maybe even more about you than about the other person.

Can you recall a love that you felt was doomed from the start? Everyone has them, and as stomachache-inducing as they may be, we can't resist dwelling on them. What did you learn about yourself from this disaster of a relationship? Probably the answer could be quite a lot. It really depends on you. You can learn a great deal from the love you feel for others.

It's probably important to mention now that when it comes to relationships — and not self-knowledge — whether the other person loves you back is crucial. I don't want people getting into marriages (for example) where they're not being loved because of the potential for self-knowledge. However, any other relationships you have already been in that weren't as loving as you wanted them to be are interesting places to search for yourself.

Now you have a good idea of who you love, why you love them, and what that says about you. You should be able to look back at your relationships and say with more certainty what you look for in others and why you admire those things. You should be able to tell which of those qualities you don't have yourself.

Making a List

Let's look back at what we have been talking about and make some assessment of our progress. By now you understand fully that a moment is the smallest meaningful amount of time in a relationship. Can you define a moment for all the relationships you have had? Try it.

Write a list — you can use the one you have been working on or start a new one. Make it as inclusive or exclusive as you like, but to the left of each name, write down a title representing the story. Then go down the list and write an emotion to the right of each name that sums up the feeling you had with the corresponding person. Now go down the list again, and in another column define the impression that person gave you.

Finally, name the trait that most attracted you. This is the final step. Now look at your list. For each name you should see a trail of logic, a method laid out for recognizing, categorizing, and absorbing positive things from those around you.

You've also got something else that is very useful: a list of things you want, ready to be obtained. This list is going to be important as you journey toward making these changes more than cosmetic. Keep it.

Here's a sample list to get you started:

Moment	Name	Impression	Feeling	Trait
True Faith	Amanda	faith	understanding	spiritual tolerance
Departure	Yoshiko	appreciation	grateful	positive outlook
In the Air	Rose	wonder	amazement	abandon

Questions and Answers: Step Four

What are the differences among feelings, impressions, and qualities?

A feeling is an emotion, something real but intangible, that you experience when you're with another person or thinking about him or her. A feeling can be something like confidence, which you might experience when you know a loved one is around. Or it can be something like awe, which you might feel in admiring the talent of a good friend.

An impression is a way of describing a complex interaction in the simplest terms. The impression you get from a person becomes apparent as you analyze each moment of your relationship. An impression can be one of organization, experience, or foolishness. Essentially, it is a way in which things are done.

A quality is a trait, an actual characteristic of another person. It is a manner of approach or a method of operation that you can recognize in someone else. Rose's quality of abandon — the ability to take pleasure in the present moment — gave her a sense of wonderment that inspired me to feel amazement in her presence. Once you have become comfortable thinking about relationships in the way this book outlines, you will often be able to consider someone and jump right to the quality that you admire in them. You will be able to tell right away what someone has that you want. Once you recognize it, you can obtain that quality simply by sublimating the concept. For example, if you admire a good listener and decide you want to be a better listener, you simply need to listen better. There is nothing else to it. You simply name and understand what you want, then you make a conscious effort to become it. Plus, you will already have a built-in role model you can look to for examples of how best to make that quality a part of your life.

What is naming things? How does this work?

Naming things is a crucial part of this process. In order to achieve anything, you have to be able to name it. You have to be able to make it real in your head in order to realize it in the world. Naming things comes easily and naturally to most people, because we think in words and so, by thinking of a thing, we usually name it automatically. However, it seems that when love gets involved, everything becomes more difficult to express. That's why I am reminding you that just looking for a feeling or an impression won't be enough. You have to be able to look at yourself seriously and say, "I want to be _____" or "I need more _____ in my life." You have to fill that blank in if you hope to make it happen.

How will naming something help me actually get it?

Once you name what you want, the quality will be on your mind. You can bring it up in conversation, ask other people about it, and be present-minded about bringing it into the way you act and what you do. Once you realize that something is important to you, you become attuned to it, in yourself and others, and you begin to see places where it will fit.

You are constantly sending messages about who your true self is by choosing people that represent certain things you like. If you do not name and define those things, you are not hearing the message you are sending and will not learn from it. If you can pin down what it is you are smitten by, you will have revealed another thing you want to see in yourself.

You say I should own my love, but I want to be loved back. Are you saying I'm wrong?

No, of course not. Everyone wants to be loved back and that is normal, but I am suggesting here that you can own love regardless of whether you are loved back.

For example, let's say you were in love with a person who was a terrible influence on you, drove you to do risky things you would normally avoid, and cheated on you with someone else. And let's say you have a wonderful and loyal spouse. Which relationship is more fulfilling? Almost certainly the second. But from which did you learn more about yourself? It's a tricky question, but the answer is that they are potentially equal.

There is a distinct difference between what makes a relationship work and what makes it worthy of analysis. A relationship that should be broken off immediately can still hold potential for you to learn from if you think about it instead of staying in it. You can learn just as much from the one who broke your heart as from the one who mended it.

How does all this translate into a better life?

If you're asking this question, you are ready for the final step.

Step Five:

Becoming Who You Already Are

You *already* are who you love. You wouldn't love the people you do if you didn't have a natural tendency toward the things you recognize as lovable in them. So how can you find ways to let these qualities express themselves in your life? Your first line of attack should, of course, be to return to analyzing the relationship itself. How did your loved one manage to be the way you admire? Given the particulars of your life, how could you adapt those techniques to work for you? See the similarities between you and the other person, and then you will see where the trait fits in your life.

If that doesn't work — maybe the other person's circumstances were too different — try this technique:

Inside Out

Imagine yourself as your ideal mate. You are an idealized version of your wife or husband, girlfriend or boyfriend. You are perfect. When you look at your significant other (your real self), you find that person desirable but somehow lacking. How? What do you recommend? How can this person you love make himself or herself more perfect, more like what he or she wants and what you want as well?

Thinking outside yourself can help you to be introspective. If you are trying to find a way to let something you have found in someone else into your own life, try talking it over with a loved one inside your head. Often, if you can imagine his or her way of thinking, you can imagine the answer to your own question.

Try calling to mind a person you know well, but who is not readily available for conversation. In your head, have an imaginary talk with that person about whatever trait you most admire in him or her. Imagine his or her responses to your inquiries.

Making It Real

By now you have a list of traits that you are looking to obtain and an idea of how you might go ahead and achieve this change. So how do you make sure you really do it? You can make use of your current relationships through the following techniques.

1. Tell People

I like to tell people when I am going to make a change, because I know that I have a harder time disappointing others than myself. This is a personal choice. Think about yourself and what you do. If you tell everyone about something great you are going to do, are you more or less likely to actually do it? That's the key here: if you don't like to disappoint others, you should tell everyone you know whatever you're going to try to change.

Sometimes it's good to tell the person you are copying; most friends, lovers, and family members would be flattered to hear something like "I decided that I want to become a more _____ person, like you are. Do you have any advice?" Their guidance can make it easier to change and can be a good motivator if you are looking for encouragement.

2. Or Don't

Maybe you like to surprise people with radical change. Only you know this about yourself, but make a decision and stick to it so that you are likely to make it happen. If you are the kind of person who loses interest unless everyone is surprised, you should keep your plans to yourself.

There are also other times you may not want to tell. For example, you may want to change something that you don't talk about with many people. Perhaps you noticed something you liked in someone that might embarrass him or her if you pointed it out. In these situations tact may be called for, and perhaps it is best to say nothing.

3. Use Your Moments as Examples

Whenever you are at an impasse in your personal progress, the best thing to do is go back to the moment that taught you the trait you are trying to acquire. Go back into your own memory and try to figure out from the clues that were there how the trait will work in your life. Use the moment as a doorway into starting the imaginary conversation we talked about, or otherwise recall the way your loved one accomplished whatever you are currently trying to do.

Take strength from the knowledge that you have love for this person because of the trait in question, and you will be able to see how the trait is already in you, waiting to come out.

4. Use Your Moments as Inspiration

Use the moments you already remember to help you keep sight of your goal. If you find yourself slipping in your resolve, remember that moment to give yourself the feeling of being in the presence of the admirable trait in question. That feeling will help you be determined in your endeavor.

Calling these moments of love to your mind will be a constant reminder that you have learned along the way and are learning still. It will bring you closer to your goals by making you mindful of them, and it will keep you focused on the meaning of your relationship.

5. Create Moments for Yourself

Come back to your moments from the past regularly, but also remember that you can create new moments for yourself. Take every opportunity you are presented with to surprise yourself. If you are feeling something should be done but notice yourself hesitating, stop thinking and just do it. Afterwards, think about why it was or wasn't the right thing to do and determine what that says about you and how you want to live your life.

One danger of introspection is the tendency not to act but to think through everything *ad infinitum*. I encourage you to think deeply about all the things in this book, but remember that in order to have moments to hold on to, you must experience things, and life is experienced through action, not thought. Thought before action can make actions more effective, and thought after action will help create meaning from events that have occurred.

Try to find and describe moments in your life as they occur. You will find that you recognize them instantaneously after a short time. This can shorten the process by giving you a kind of distance that allows you to learn right away upon meeting someone what can potentially make them important to you. The easier this becomes, the easier it'll be for you to like people and enjoy their company because you'll understand all the different ways people can teach you.

6. Name Things

Vague goals cannot be achieved. You must put a name to each thing you want, each trait you admire, and each mannerism you appreciate in order to absorb them. You have to add these things to your self-definition. If you are in love with a person's sensitivity, then you are, among other things, a sensitive person. You must be, or you wouldn't love that person for that trait. So how can you become more sensitive? You don't need to become anything — you already are sensitive, but you simply need to express the sensitivity that is part of you and is already important to you. You can use your relationship as an instructive example, and soon you will find that you have grown considerably in this way.

7. Own Your Love

I can't stress this enough. Your love is your business and relates to you. Find what you want in yourself by looking into others. After all, you do it anyway, and you may as well be learning something from it.

Every time you feel love, you are making a statement about who you are and what you like. You have to come to the realization that love is something in you, about you, and for you. It has to do with other people, but remembering that it comes from you will be a compass, always orienting you toward self-discovery.

This is useful all across your life, but is especially so after a relationship is over and you are trying to get some distance from it. You can separate yourself from some of the sadness or feelings of loss that might set in by looking at the love you felt as an excellent, exciting, and informative part of you — a message *from* you, *to* you, and most importantly, *about* you.

8. Learn from Other Sources

There are a number of other sources that can be useful examples to you, outside the realm of human relationships. You can learn certain things from characters in books or movies, from stories you hear about other people, and from religious stories. But remember that these sources are fundamentally different and have to be translated in order to be applied to your life. Not everything will necessarily fit. Unlike your own loves, which are tailored to your own needs by definition, other sources have to be decoded and turned from example into the underlying universal statement. Then a decision must be made as to whether you agree with the statement.

Of course, you can learn things from books, as they are written by humans with the intent to communicate and constitute some kind of relationship between the writer and reader. But books too have their limits; even this book, which has tried to be as open-ended as possible, can't tell you everything.

Be as objective as you can be — evaluate every new piece of information you receive on its own merits and determine the extent to which you can trust it as legitimate information.

9. Analyze Your Own Behavior

We touched on this in the imaginary conversation. Try improving yourself from the outside in. Think about what other people might want to see in you. Not just any people, but the people you find most important: those you love.

After some social interaction — say, a conversation with someone you care about, or a night spent with a close friend — try to recreate the scene, not only from your perspective but as you imagine the other people in the room might have seen it. This will help you understand that your behavior was communicated to the other people in the room, and you will start to realize what you communicated. You will then have a starting place for analyzing whether what you are communicating is your intended message.

Questions and Answers: *Step Five*

What if I know what I want, but I just can't be it?

We have to admit there are things beyond our will to control them. For example, no amount of wanting it is going to make you the Queen of France. Some traits may be out of your reach, at least for now.

For example, I knew a girl back in high school who was admirably focused. She always seemed to be "on task." I couldn't do that; I was always bored or fussing around. I decided that I wanted her resolve and I tried hard to be more focused, but even to this day I am a lot less focused than I wish I were — though I have to admit, I am more focused than I was then. This is going to happen. As long as you are growing and making progress, you should be proud and hopeful. There is no guarantee that you can be everything you want to be, nor is there anything to say that if you can't quite make something happen now, it won't happen for you later.

You are going to find traits that you can't quite get your mind all the way around, but knowing your limitations — and being able to deal with them properly — is a great benefit, as well. Perhaps this is not quite so transformative, but it is equally useful. If you come across something that you cannot seem to get, try to figure out a way to make up for it in some other way that you can accomplish.

How can having an "imaginary conversation" with someone be helpful?

Our mental depictions often reveal quite a lot of what we think about other people. Use your imagination and have an entire exchange in your head. Address the other person and have them answer you as you imagine they would. You can talk things over with them and ascertain how you would imagine them advising you. This is a trick, of course, because you are really advising yourself.

That's the whole idea: when you love, you love yourself. When you learn, you teach yourself. When you change, you change yourself. Everything about you is created *by* you. You fall in love to tell yourself you like something. If you recognize it and name it, you can obtain it. If you imagine the other person in your head, you'll find a way to obtain it that makes sense to you.

You said to relive moments, but then you say I have to act on them. Which is it?

It's both. Act, then think, then act based on the thinking. Which is to say, make sure you don't live only in your head and memories. Investigation is inherently good; the more you know, the more capable you are of making good decisions. But simply being informed doesn't necessarily mean you will always be right. You also have to pay attention to what your body is telling you, and most of all, you have to act. The worst decision is the decision never made.

When you love, you love yourself. When you learn, you teach yourself. When you change, you change yourself.

Conclusion

*E*very lesson in this book is developed from the normal ways people see themselves and others. You may already use some of the techniques I have outlined without thinking about them, but learning to recognize these ideas and name the things you want is essential. As you name things ever more effectively, you will be able to make a lot of positive changes in your life.

This method is a formulation of things I learned by paying close attention to those I loved and taking from them cues for myself. I was a born student, and I have asserted all along in this book that life is a free and always-open classroom, where you don't have to pay tuition — just your dues — and your teachers are the very people you love, whether or not they know it.

Live a more thoughtful and analytic version of your life. You can. Using the techniques you've learned, you will more easily recognize qualities that are better for you and that will improve your life. Pay attention to the people you love because they are all you have for examples or critics. The only people we have to please are ourselves and the people we have chosen to love. Because, in the end, they are one and the same: we are who we love.

About the Author

T. J. Kupper was born in Connecticut and educated in Los Angeles. He hopes this book will help you to think more effectively about yourself and to become those things that you admire.